To

_____

From

_____

Date

_____

THE SATURDAY
EVENING POST

Grandma's Memories
of Growing Up

A Keepsake Record Book

HARVEST HOUSE PUBLISHERS

EUGENE, OREGON

Cover and Interior Design by Garborg Design Works, Savage, Minnesota

All illustrations © SEPS. Licensed by Curtis Licensing, Indianapolis, IN. All Rights Reserved.

Harvest House Publishers has made every effort to trace the ownership of all poems and quotes. In the event of a question arising from the use of a poem or quote, we regret any error made and will be pleased to make the necessary correction in future editions of this book.

Grandma's Memories of Growing Up

Copyright © 2011 by Harvest House Publishers

Published by Harvest House Publishers
Eugene, Oregon 97402
www.harvesthousepublishers.com

ISBN 978-0-7369-2982-0

Printed in China

12 13 14 15 16 17 18 19 / LP / 10 9 8 7 6 5 4 3

This memory book is created by

_____

with great love for

_____

Light tomorrow with today.

ELIZABETH BARRETT BROWNING

_____

God sends children for another purpose than merely to keep up the race—to enlarge our hearts; and to make us unselfish and full of kindly sympathies and affections; to give our souls higher aims; to call out all our faculties to extended enterprise and exertion; and to bring round our firesides bright faces, happy smiles, and loving, tender hearts.

MARY HOWITT

Special Delivery

When and where were you born? _____

_____

_____

What is your full maiden name? _____

_____

_____

Did you have a nickname? _____

Who was there to welcome you to the world? _____

_____

_____

_____

Share a story you've heard about your birth. _____

_____

_____

_____

_____

_____

Those who loved you and were helped by you will remember you when forget-me-nots have withered. Carve your name on hearts, not on marble.

CHARLES H. SPURGEON

Heaven lies about us in our infancy.

WILLIAM WORDSWORTH

Family Story

Who were your parents and where were they from? _____

_____

_____

_____

_____

_____

Who else was a part of your family? _____

_____

_____

_____

Where did your family originate from? _____

_____

_____

_____

_____

A happy family is but an earlier heaven.

Sir John Bowring

How did your family make you feel safe? _____

_____

_____

_____

_____

_____

_____

_____

_____

_____

_____

_____

_____   *Our home joys are the most delightful earth*
                                                affords, and the joy of parents in their
_____   *children is the most holy joy of humanity.*
                                                It makes their hearts pure and good, it lifts
_____   *men up to their Father in heaven.*

JOHANN PESTALOZZI

All About You

Which three words best describe your personality as a kid? _____

_____

_____

What significant events in history were going on during the years you were young? _____

_____

_____

_____

_____

_____

_____

_____

_____

_____

_____

_____

Every child born into the world
is a new thought of God, an
ever-fresh and radiant possibility.
KATE DOUGLAS WIGGIN

Share a fun memory you have of your childhood. _____

_____

_____

_____

_____

_____

_____

_____

_____

_____

_____

A good heart,
benevolent feelings,
and a balanced mind,
lie at the foundation
of character.

JOHN TODD

_____

_____

Growing Up

When did you first feel grown up? _____

_____

_____

What was your first or favorite job? _____

_____

_____

_____

What did you buy with the first money you earned or saved? _____

_____

_____

_____

_____

Describe one of the biggest or hardest decisions you ever had to make.

How'd you make it? _____

_____

_____

The great thing in this world is not so much where
we are, but in what direction we are moving.

OLIVER WENDELL HOLMES

Nature gives to every time and season some beauties of its own; and from morning to night, as from the cradle to the grave, is but a succession of changes so gentle and easy that we can scarcely mark their progress.

CHARLES DICKENS

_____

_____

_____

_____

_____

_____

_____

_____

_____

_____

_____

_____

Dreams and Passions

What did you daydream about as a young girl? _____
_____
_____

What made you happiest? _____
_____
_____
_____
_____

_____

_____

_____

_____

_____

_____

*There is always one moment
in childhood when the door
opens and lets the future in.*

<small>GRAHAM GREENE</small>

Who were your heroes and why? _____

_____

_____

_____

_____

_____

_____

_____

_____

What did you wish for when you blew out your birthday candles as a girl? _____

_____

_____

_____

_____

_____

Youth is the opportunity to do something and to become somebody.
THEODORE MUNGER

13

School Days

Describe your childhood school. _____

_____

_____

_____

_____

What were your favorite/least favorite subjects in school? _____

_____

_____

_____

Which activities outside of the classroom were your favorites?

Did you do sports or choir? Were you in the school play? _____

_____

_____

_____

_____

_____

Children have more need of models than of critics.

JOSEPH JOUBERT

How did a teacher or mentor make

a difference in your life? _____

_____

_____

_____

_____

_____

_____

_____

_____

_____

_____

_____

_____

_____

_____

_____

*To make knowledge
valuable, you must have
the cheerfulness of wisdom.
Goodness smiles to the last.*

RALPH WALDO EMERSON

A Stylish Gal

What clothes were in fashion when you were a kid? _____

_____

_____

_____

_____

_____

_____

How did you and your friends express your personal style? _____

_____

_____

_____

_____

_____

_____

_____

Don't judge each day by the harvest
you reap, but by the seeds you plant.
ROBERT LOUIS STEVENSON

What trends or sayings were popular when you were young? _____

_____

_____

_____

_____

_____

_____

_____

_____

_____

_____

_____

_____

We are shaped
and fashioned by
what we love.

JOHANN WOLFGANG VON GOETHE

Sparks of Creativity

Tell me about something you made or created. _____

_____

_____

_____

What kind of music inspired you? What about today? _____

_____

_____

_____

What were your favorite books to read? _____

_____

_____

_____

_____

How did you express your creativity as a child? _____

_____

What we learn with pleasure, we never forget.

ALFRED MERCIER

_____

18

Describe your favorite hobbies as a kid and now. _____

The plays of natural lively children are the infancy of art. Children live in a world of imagination and feeling. They invest the most insignificant object with any form they please, and see in it whatever they wish to see.

ADAM OEHLENSCHLAGER

Nature's Playground

When you were in the great outdoors as a kid,

what did you love to do? Swim, hike, garden?

_____

_____

_____

_____

_____

_____

Describe your favorite outdoor places

and spaces then and now. _____

_____

_____

_____

_____

_____

Nature is beautiful, always beautiful! Every little flake of snow is a perfect crystal, and they fall together as gracefully as if fairies of the air caught water drops and made them into artificial flowers to garland the wings of the wind!

Lydia Child

If you could spend time in the mountains or at the beach, which would you choose? _____

_____

What would you do there? _____

_____

_____

_____

_____

_____

What is your favorite flower or tree? _____

_____

_____

_____

The fairest flower in the garden
of creation is a young mind,
offering and unfolding itself
to the influence of the divine
wisdom, as the heliotrope turns
its sweet blossoms to the sun.

JAMES EDWARD SMITH

Friends Forever

Who have been some of your dearest friends over the years, and what do you love about them?

_____

_____

_____

_____

_____

_____

_____

What qualities do you think make the best kind of friend? _____

_____

_____

_____

_____

_____

Every house where love abides and friendship
is a guest, is surely home, and home, sweet
home; for there the heart can rest.

HENRY VAN DYKE

What did you and your friends like to do on a sunny day? On a rainy day?

_____

_____

_____

_____

_____

_____

_____

_____

_____

_____

_____

_____

_____

_____

*Of all the things which wisdom provides
to make life entirely happy, much the
greatest is the possession of friendship.*

EPICURUS

Animal Companions

What pets did you have during your life? Which was your favorite? _____

_____

_____

_____

_____

Was there an animal you always wanted but never got to have? _____

_____

_____

_____

Were there farm animals or friends' pets that you enjoyed? _____

_____

_____

_____

_____

_____

*There is only one happiness in
life, to love and be loved.*

GEORGE SAND

Is there a funny or comforting story you have to share about an animal's unconditional love?

_____

_____

_____

_____

_____

_____

_____

_____

_____

_____

_____

_____

_____

Stay is a charming word in a friend's vocabulary.

AMOS BRONSON ALCOTT

Hometown Memories

What did you love about your hometown? _____

_____

_____

_____

_____

_____

_____

_____

Describe your childhood house, room, yard, and neighborhood. _____

_____

_____

_____

_____

_____

You will find as you look back upon life that the moments when you have really lived are the moments when you have done things in the spirit of love.

Henry Drummond

What was your first home as an adult like? Why did you live there? _____

_____

_____

_____

_____

If you could choose to live anywhere in the world, where would it be? _____

_____

_____

_____

_____

_____

_____

_____

_____

Without hearts there is no home.

GEORGE BYRON

27

Fun and Games

What games did you play as a child? _____

_____

_____

_____

Describe a game you played with your children when they were young. _____

_____

_____

_____

_____

_____

_____

_____

_____

_____

The laughter of girls is, and ever was,
among the delightful sounds of earth.

THOMAS DE QUINCEY

28

What is your favorite way to stay active?

_____

_____

_____

_____

_____

_____

_____

Which season of life has been the most fun? Why? _____

_____

_____

_____

_____

_____

_____

_____

_____

_____

The joys I have possessed are ever mine;
out of thy reach, behind eternity, hid in
the sacred treasure of the past, but blest
remembrance brings them hourly back.

JOHN DRYDEN

Gather Together

What was the conversation about at your childhood dinner table? _____

_____

_____

_____

Share a mealtime prayer or tradition you had as a child or as an adult. _____

_____

_____

_____

_____

_____

_____

A dining room table
with children's eager,
hungry faces around
it ceases to be a mere
dining room table and
becomes an altar.

SIMEON STRUNSKY

_____

_____

What is your recipe for a happy life? _____

_____

_____

_____

_____

What is one of your favorite foods? Favorite recipes? _____

_____

_____

_____

_____

_____

_____

Home is the resort of love, of joy, of peace, and plenty, where supporting and
supported, polished friends and dearest relatives mingle into bliss.

JAMES THOMSON

Good Times

Why are you glad that you grew up when you did? _____

_____

_____

_____

_____

What made your family, community, and the country special when you were young? _____

_____

_____

_____

_____

_____

_____

_____

_____

A good laugh is
sunshine in a house.

WILLIAM MAKEPEACE THACKERAY

The cheerful live longest in years,
and afterwards in our regards.
Cheerfulness is the off-shoot of goodness.

CHRISTIAN NESTELL BOVEE

_____

_____

_____

_____

_____

_____

_____

_____

What do you think defines the "good life"? _____

_____

_____

_____

_____

_____

_____

Love Makes the World Go Round

When did you know you were falling in love? _____

_____

_____

_____

_____

What do you remember most about your wedding? _____

_____

_____

_____

_____

_____

_____

_____

_____

_____

Perfect love sometimes does not come till the first grandchild.

WELSH PROVERB

Describe the most romantic gift you received or gave? _____

_____

_____

_____

_____

_____

_____

Share something you've learned about loving others.

_____

_____

_____

_____

_____

_____

_____

As dew to the blossom, and bud to the bee, as the
scent to the rose, are those memories to me.

Amelia B. Welby

35

Spirit of Adventure

What was your biggest adventure as a kid? _____

_____

_____

_____

_____

_____

What adventure do you still want to enjoy? _____

_____

_____

_____

_____

_____

_____

_____

*Curiosity is as much the parent of
attention, as attention is of memory.*

Describe a time when your curiosity got
you in trouble or led to an adventure.

_____

_____

_____

_____

_____

_____

If you could take your grandchildren on one great adventure, what would that adventure

look like?_____

_____

_____

_____

_____

_____

Children and genius have the same master-organ in common—inquisitiveness. Let
childhood have its way, and as it began where genius begins it may find what genius finds.

Edward Bulwer-Lytton

Faith and Joy

When did you experience the deepest sense of joy as a child? _____

_____

_____

_____

_____

_____

_____

Where did you feel safest or the closest to God? _____

_____

_____

_____

_____

_____

_____

My soul blesses the great Father, every day, that he
has gladdened the earth with little children.

MARY HOWITT

A cheerful look brings
joy to the heart,
and good news gives
health to the bones.

THE BOOK OF PROVERBS

_____

_____

_____

_____

_____

What inspires your faith and sense of hope? _____

_____

_____

_____

_____

_____

_____

_____

_____

Memories and Legacies

Do you have a special memory of your grandparents and parents? _____

_____

_____

_____

_____

What daily ritual or routine with your family gave you comfort? _____

_____

_____

_____

_____

_____

_____

_____

There is a magic in that little word,
home; it is a mystic circle that
surrounds comforts and virtues never
known beyond its hallowed limits.

ROBERT SOUTHEY

As a girl, what did you enjoy doing with your mom?

_____

_____

_____

_____

_____

_____

Describe your favorite family tradition or the memory of a special gathering or holiday.

_____

_____

_____

_____

_____

_____

_____

_____

_____

Memory, the daughter of attention, is the teeming mother of knowledge.

MARTIN TUPPER

Becoming a Parent and Grandparent

How many children did you have? _____

_____

_____

_____

_____

What are your fondest memories of being a parent? _____

_____

_____

_____

_____

_____

When you got the news that you were going to be a grandparent,

what did you think and feel? _____

_____

_____

_____

Children are the hands by which we take hold of heaven.

HENRY WARD BEECHER

Grandchildren are the crowning glory of the aged;
Parents are the pride of their children.

THE BOOK OF PROVERBS

_____

_____

_____

_____

_____

_____

_____

_____

What is the greatest joy of being a grandparent?

_____

_____

_____

_____

_____

_____

_____

A Grandparent's Wisdom

Share wisdom or a life lesson that you want to pass on. _____

_____

_____

_____

_____

_____

What would you say is the secret to a good life? _____

_____

_____

_____

_____

_____

Pass along some words of wisdom that your parents or grandparents gave to you. _____

_____

_____

_____

_____

There is not a man or woman, however poor they may be, but have it in their power, by the grace of God, to leave behind them the grandest thing on earth, character; and their children might rise up after them and thank God that their mother was a pious woman, or their father a pious man.

Norman Macleod

The truest greatness
lies in being kind,
the truest wisdom
in a happy mind.

ELLA WHEELER WILCOX

_____

_____

_____

_____

_____

_____

_____

What is your biggest prayer and hope for your grandchild? _____

A Letter to Your Grandchild

What do you want your grandchildren and future generations to know about you, about your
family, and about the special days of your childhood? _____

_____

_____

_____

_____

_____

_____

_____

_____

_____

_____

_____

_____

_____

I have often thought what a melancholy world this would be
without children; and what an inhuman world, without the aged.

SAMUEL COLERIDGE

The heart hath its own memory, like the mind,
And in it are enshrined
The precious keepsakes, into which is wrought
The giver's loving thought.

HENRY WADSWORTH LONGFELLOW

Childhood itself is scarcely more lovely
than a cheerful, kindly, sunshiny old age.

Lydia Child